Pittsburgh

...Views into the 21st Century

GW01005478

Photography by Joel B. Levinson,
Susan Nega and others

. . . .

Photography: Joel B. Levinson,
Susan Nega and others

. . . .

Introduction: Robert Gangewere

. . . .

Cover photograph: Joel B. Levinson

. . . .

Pittsburgh: Views Into the 21st Century

Pittsburgh is a city with a story to tell. Photographers, artists, and travelers see that immediately. Visually exciting, Pittsburgh had a dramatic colonial history, a heroic part of the American Industrial Age, and after the Second World War, an amazing "renaissance" transforming this smoky milltown into a city constantly admired for the quality of its urban life.

Arriving at Pittsburgh from the West, the traveler comes through the Fort Pitt Tunnel and is suddenly confronted by a cityscape that leaps to the eye. "It is the only city in America with an entrance," says *The New York Times*.

Apparent at a glance is Pittsburgh's reason for existence—the three rivers which make it a transportation hub in the mountains of western Pennsylvania. In the 18th century it was the Gateway to the West, since the Ohio flows 980 miles to the Mississippi and then south to the Gulf of Mexico, or north to the Missouri, and Northwest.

The Iron City of the early 19th century became the Steel City of the post Civil War era and the 20th century. Pittsburgh's many bridges reveal a history of engineering and design, and its many hills and valleys contain stories of ethnic populations. Now Pittsburgh enters the 21st century with a vigor and excitement that builds on the region's strengths—people, the educational and medical environment, arts and recreational attractions. The modern city, erected on the site of the world's most famous milltown, tells a story of partnership between government and private business in redirecting the city's economic energy and literally changing the look of the city.

The Pittsburgh experience for the visitor, however brief, has several levels. First, there is the surprise of "the Arrival." The view of the city as one emerges from the Fort Pitt Tunnel never fails to please. Second, there is the City itself, highly concentrated placement of the 19th century buildings next to post-modern architecture in a reasonable, easily grasped way. Next there are the Neighborhoods, marked by Old World churches and ethnic stability, with a strong sense of place.

There is a second city, the university town—Oakland, with its museums, educational and medical facilities, and pleasurable park lands. These complexes are shaping Pittsburgh for the 21st century. There are many Pleasures of the City, urbane and familial, from the Symphony to the Zoo, from the Arts Festival to the Three Rivers Regatta, from sculling on the river to cross country skiing. The city is a strong Sports City. Finally, the section of this book entitled Hidden Treasures of the City tries to convey just a few of its jewels.

In these photographs the pace and variety of Pittsburgh are felt. It is a city of under 400,000 residents, which acts as a regional Mecca for millions in Pennsylvania, Ohio, and West Virginia. People who love its big city style, traditions, sophisticated pleasures, and positive outlook toward life during the 21st century.

—Robert Gangewere

A view of Pittsburgh coming through the Fort Pitt Tunnels.

Joel B. Levinson (JBL)

JBL

Sunrise launch of hot air balloons over the city

Norman Schumm

As sun sets, the city turns golden.

Coming to the City

Join us in exploring a view between the rivers as seen from its many approaches. For those living on Mt. Washington, a place from which the best views of the city can be had, the city's two inclines (the Monongahela and Duquesne) are more than just the city's biggest attractions; they are a way to get to work.

JBL

From the east at sunrise the city glows with a golden light. The remains of the steel industry (see also page 94) that built the city are still here in the foreground, but so is the new technology center just behind.

JBL

From the South and West one trip through the Fort Pitt Tunnels and "presto", the city magically appears with a "WOW!"

From the West along the Ohio River, the city becomes framed by the majestic arches of the West End Bridge.

Susan L. Nega (SLN)

From the North, the road snakes through the city's many hills and valleys, and erupts in grandeur as it crosses the Allegheny River.

JBL

Port Authority Light Rail transit to the city

Light Rail Transit becomes subway in downtown

13

Travel by car, bus, balloon, boat, Amtrak rail, barge, light rail transit, or by plane, the city is always an awesome sight. The rivers are like outstretched arms waiting to welcome all.

Water taxis to, from, and within the city

Port Authority Transit buses travel throughout the city.

Excursion boat "Down by the Riverside"

JBL

The Pittsburgh International Airport

Many people who come to Pittsburgh arrive at the midfield terminal of the airport 20 miles from the Golden Triangle. It is one of the most modern airports in the country, with a mall of unique shops and eateries for the traveler. The midfield terminal is connected to the landside terminal by an underground people mover. Soon the city center will be linked to the terminal by a limited access busway.

JBL

JBL

SLN

Many people come to the city because of their desire to be a part of the hot air balloon mania that grips the city all summer long. At Regatta time, balloons lift off daily. Because of the hills and rivers, the city has air flows that send a hot air balloon north one day, the next day east, and the next day south or west.

SLN

JBL

Some arrive by crossing the Smithfield Street Bridge (1883).

Many barges and crews visit the city.

River movement of goods built Pittsburgh throughout the 19th and 20th centuries. It is still a vital link to economic stability for the area as the region enters the 21st century.

JBL

JBL

SLN

SLN

JBL

JBL

The City

No matter how you come to the city, you will find its magic. It is a blend of the antique structures dwarfed by modern tall buildings that house corporate headquarters, law offices, financial institutions and services, telecommunications, architectural firms, advertising concerns, as well as the regional and federal courts and administrative offices. Pittsburgh continues to expand as a cultural center for the Tri-State Area with Benedum Hall, Heinz Hall, Byham Theater, art galleries and more in the Golden Triangle. It has high rise apartment buildings, parks, parklets, clubs, docking areas, full-service shopping establishments, including Kaufmann's Department Store, Saks Fifth Avenue, Lazarus, Brooks Brothers, and many more. Within a fifteen minute walk are the Andy Warhol Museum, Carnegie Science Center, Pittsburgh Children's Museum, as well as the sports and entertainment focus of Three Rivers Stadium and Civic Arena. Close to the Convention Center are the new Senator John Heinz Pittsburgh Regional History Center, hotels, Boardwalk restaurants, and Strip District markets and shops.

JBL

From above, the Civic Arena appears as a flying saucer that has landed among Pittsburgh's tall buildings.

Pittsburgh from the North Shore

JBL

The steeples of Pittsburgh churches have influenced the architecture of some of the city's prominent and newer structures, like Fifth Avenue Place and the buildings of PPG Place.

PPG Tower and Fifth Avenue Place

JBL

Smithfield United Church (1925)

JBL

Trinity Episcopal Church (1872)

JBL

St. John the Baptist Ukrainian Church (1895) on Pittsburgh's South Side

JBL

Looking over Mt. Washington neighborhood into the Golden Triangle

JBL

Mellon Park, with parking garage beneath

JBL

The atrium of Two Mellon Bank Center, formerly the Union Trust Building

SLN

Fort Pitt Blockhouse (1794) in Point State Park

JBL

First Lutheran Church

Civic Arena

SLN

*Duquesne University on the bluff and
Golden Triangle beyond*

JBL

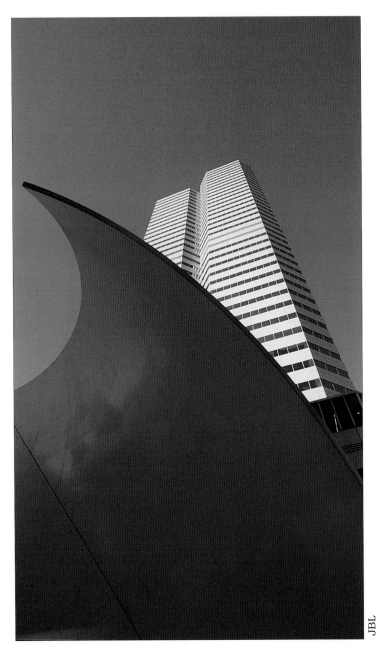

Early 1900s First Avenue buildings against unusual architecture and design of the 1960s

JBL

Northlight sculpture (D. Von Schlegell) in front of the Oxford Building

Turn-of-the-century wharf buildings on Fort Pitt Boulevard

JBL

Dollar Savings Bank protector on Fourth Avenue

SLN

View coming down from Troy Hill

29

Reflections in the PPG Building

SLN

Kaufmann's Clock

JBL

PPG Wintergarden

JBL

30

Pittsburgh is the City of Bridges.

JBL

JBL

*Bridge of Sighs between the county
courthouse and the old jail*

JBL

St. Benedict the Moor in the Hill District

32

PPG Plaza glows with luminaries during Light Up Night

SLN

Oakland: Pittsburgh's Second City

Home to Pittsburgh's two largest universities, world-renowned medical centers, cultural attractions, apartment and residential living, and Schenley Park, a four-season experience. The Oakland area developed around the end of the 19th century when Mary Schenley gave to the city the park that bears her name. Andrew Carnegie stepped in with the Museum, Free Library and Carnegie Institute of Technology. Phipps added the Conservatory (1893) which has flower shows year round. Shops and eateries can be found on South Craig Street, by The Sarah Scaife Gallery of The Carnegie.

JBL

On a two-block area just outside
the entrance to The Carnegie's
Sarah Scaife Gallery are South
Craig Street shops. Besides eating
establishments of diverse menus,
there are unique shops selling
clothing, used books, cards and
gifts, comic books, art, and jewelry.

Watermelon Blues

Macondo

Callaban Books

JBL

Children's Hospital

JBL

University of Pittsburgh Medical Center

JBL

By the Stephen Foster Sculpture

37

SLN

Schenley Park Skating Rink

JBL

Phipps Conservatory

JBL

Botany Building (c. 1900) at Phipps Conservatory

Phipps Conservatory (1893) features botanical displays and four seasonal flower shows.

JBL

Oakland as seen from the South Side

Westinghouse Memorial (French & Fjelde, 1930) bathes Schenley Park with its rainbows

JBL

Carnegie Mellon University

Since its inception, Carnegie Mellon University has been internationally recognized as the educational and research leader in technical and management curricula in the fields of Civil, Chemical, and Mechanical Engineering, and Applied Sciences. Today, Carnegie Mellon is considered the foremost university in Computer Science. Beyond technology, the drama, music, and art departments have many entertainment and art celebrities on their alumni rosters.

CMU buggy races

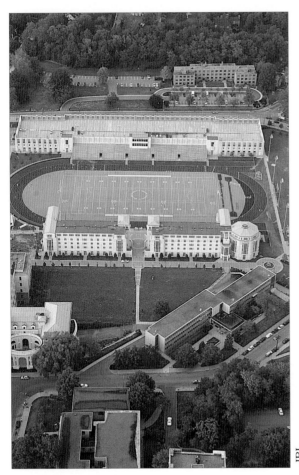

Gesling Stadium; part of the new CMU campus

Mellon Institute

Hamerschlag Hall (formerly Machinery Hall, 1912) and Computer Research Center, Wein Hall

JBL

The Carnegie

The Carnegie, a great museum and library complex founded by Andrew Carnegie in 1895, was the historic core for cultural growth in Oakland. Outside the entrance to this palace of culture are symbolic sculptures, including one of Shakespeare.

JBL

JBL

SLN

Entrance to the Carnegie Museum (1895) is through Sarah Scaife Gallery

JBL

JBL

JBL

JBL

Oakland has a lot of green spaces surrounding the library and the University of Pittsburgh's Cathedral of Learning. When the weather is mild the parks are filled with people who have taken their studying to the open air. In the winter, the same people find enjoyment in those parts of Schenley Park turned white, like those seen here cross-country skiing on the golf course, or sled riding near Heinz Chapel.

JBL

Reflections in Mervis Hall, location of the Joseph M. Katz Graduate School of Business

University of Pittsburgh

Looking west to the Golden Triangle from the University of Pittsburgh's Cathedral of Learning, one can see the vast medical complex for which Pittsburgh has reached national acclaim in medical research and transplant surgery. Within a six-block radius one can find hospitals like Magee Women's, Children's Hospital, Western Psychiatric, and the University of Pittsburgh Medical Center. UPMC includes Eye and Ear, Montefiore, Falk Clinic, and Presbyterian Hospitals, as well as the University's Medical and Dental Colleges.

JBL

Studying inside the Cathedral of Learning

JBL

Sled riding in front of Heinz Chapel

The English Room, one of many nationality rooms in the Cathedral of Learning

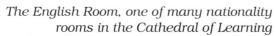

SLN

University of Pittsburgh's Cathedral of Learning

JBL

City Attractions

When one leaves the attractions in the downtown area, such as the symphony, ballet, performing arts, outdoor activities at Point State Park, and Pittsburgh's second city, Oakland, they find other points of interest spread throughout the city. North Side has the Warhol Museum, Carnegie Science Center, National Aviary, and Allegheny Complex including Carnegie's first free library in the country. East Liberty has the Pittsburgh Zoo and the old Motor Square Garden. The amusement parks stretch east along the Monongahela River and east of Ligonier, toward Frank Lloyd Wright's Fallingwater. Point Breeze has the Frick Art & Historical Center. Immediately south of the Golden Triangle is the Station Square Complex.

JBL

July 4th celebration at the Point

SLN

Concert at Civic Arena with the roof open and fireworks outside

Ballet at Benedum Center

JBL

JBL

Heinz Hall for Performing Arts

SLN

Dancing in the Grand Lobby of Heinz Hall

Station Square

Station Square is a favorite spot for visitors and Pittsburghers alike. In the fall the Columbus Day parade crosses the Smithfield Street Bridge. A ride on the Monongahela Incline takes you to Mt. Washington for a spectacular view of the city, and just as grand is a relaxing riverside view near the railcar shops.

Station Square is a short walk across the historic Smithfield Street Bridge (1883) from the Golden Triangle. Through the guidance of the Pittsburgh History & Landmarks Foundation, this turn-of-the-century (20th) railroad station has been transformed into striking, attractive office spaces with a wonderful dining and shopping complex. The Gateway Clipper Fleet docks adjacent to the complex, and an open-air entertainment amphitheater sits nearby.

Grand Concourse restaurant is in the P&LE Railroad Landmarks Building (1898).

The sea lions at play in the children's zoo

SLN

Richard Kolson

The Pittsburgh Zoo features natural habitats for the animals.

Holiday parade on Grant Street

The Pittsburgh Children's Museum is located in the old Post Office building in Landmark Square. A sculpture garden featuring historic pieces of Pittsburgh history include the Manchester Bridge Portals (1915), which connected the Point to lower North Side. Every year the Children's Festival is held here and throughout Allegheny Square. The National Aviary is close by in Allegheny West Park.

JBL

SLN

SLN

One of the fastest-growing sports in the area is rowing on the Allegheny. Each year the city plays host to the Head of the Ohio Rowing Regatta. Most crews start from Herrs Island and end at the Point.

JBL

JBL

59

Amusement Parks

There are basically three amusement parks in the area: Kennywood Park in W. Mifflin, Sandcastle water park on the Monongahela River in Homestead, and Idlewild Park in Ligonier, about 35 miles east on Route 30, where kids have their own kind of park, and adults can enjoy being young again.

The Thunderbolt wooden rollercoaster

Lost Kennywood with the Steel Phantom lurking behind

Sandcastle water park in Homestead

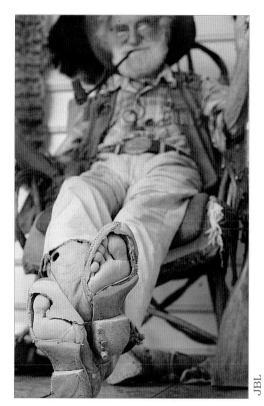

Idlewild Park in Ligonier

Neighborhood Trolley in Idlewild Park

Clayton, the beautifully restored Victorian home of industrialist Henry Clay Frick, is part of the Frick Art & Historical Center in Point Breeze. Also on the grounds are The Frick Art Museum (1969), built to house Helen Clay Frick's collection of fine and decorative arts, the Carriage Museum, Greenhouse, and lush gardens.

SLN

Dining room in Clayton House

Clayton House

JBL

The Andy Warhol Museum was opened by The Carnegie in 1994. Located on the North Side, it features an extensive collection of Warhol's art and archives. A Pittsburgh native, Andy Warhol graduated from Carnegie Institute of Technology, worked at Horne's, and became one of the most influential American artists of the 20th century.

Silver Clouds, Andy Warhol Museum

The Andy Warhol Museum

The **Carnegie Science Center** and submarine, USS Requin, lie on the North Shore, just a couple hundred yards from Three Rivers Stadium, and just a short walk across the Duquesne Bridge from the Point. Here kids get to interact with hands-on exhibits, see a fantastic train display, or a movie in the Rangos Omnimax Theater.

Miniature Railroad

Hands-on exhibits

64

The Carnegie Science Center and the city

JBL

Pittsburgh Neighborhoods

Pittsburgh neighborhoods stretch out in all directions. Some are tucked along the city's hillsides, in valleys, balanced precariously atop overlooks, or bordering its many parks. Many, like Bloomfield, Polish Hill, Troy Hill, to name a few, have strong ethnic backbones that date back generations.

JBL

Homes on top of Spring Hill, with the city in the background

North Side. A short ten-minute walk from the Golden Triangle is Old Allegheny, now known as North Side. Allegheny General Hospital is the focal point of the area. Houses on the Mexican War streets date back to the late 19th century. North Side is the home of the National Aviary, Pittsburgh Children's Museum, Allegheny West Park, Andy Warhol Museum, Allegheny Center, and North Shore office complex.

South Side flats with the Birmingham Bridge in the background

JBL

SLN

SLN

Bloomfield shines at night on Liberty Avenue. This neighborhood thrives with many local businesses and a strong ethnic community. Close by, Ritter's Diner is a favorite stop for locals and passers-through.

East Liberty is just east of Oakland and Shadyside. The Joy of Life sculpture (Cantini, 1969) sits outside the Carnegie Library and Presbyterian Cathedral, part of East Liberty Mall.

JBL

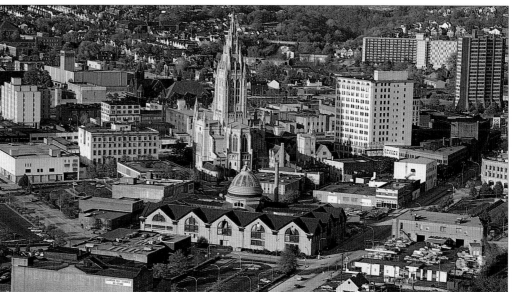

JBL

East End homes

East End homes

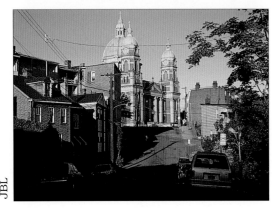

Polish Hill

South Side Hillside

72

Neighborhoods are not only places where people live and shop. They become gathering spots for all kinds of activities. Schenley Park abuts Squirrel Hill, Shadyside, and Oakland. The Strip District abuts Polish Hill, Northside, and Lawrenceville.

Smokey City Folk Festival

Shopping on Ellsworth Avenue

Nightlife in the Strip District

Technology/Industry in Pittsburgh

Pittsburgh grew up as a steel town. Much of the steel operations have left the area, but with the steel there was Heinz Foods. Heinz remains. Its slow-pouring ketchup is enshrined in a neon sign at its plant just across the Sixteenth Street Bridge. Pittsburgh's Technology Center has grown up on the site of some of the old steel mills that built Pittsburgh. Pictured here is one of the remaining steel servicing facilities in Homestead. Parts of the Edgar Thompson steel works near Braddock have been remodeled with a new continuous caster. The city, through its strong university research, has become a center for robot, medical, and software technology which has lead to high technology companies springing up throughout the area.

74

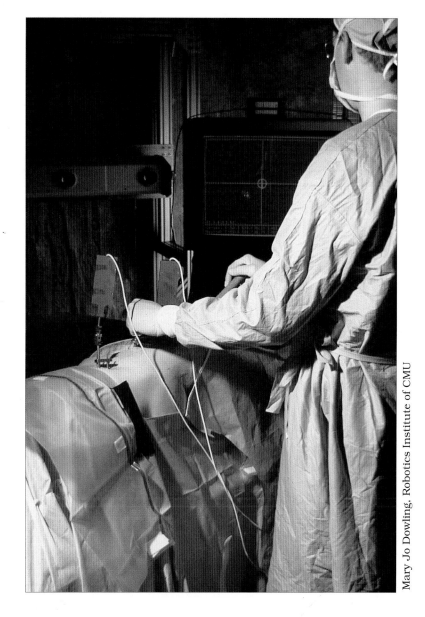

Mary Jo Dowling, Robotics Institute of CMU

Mary Jo Dowling, Robotics Institute of CMU

Pittsburgh is a leader in medical and robotics technology. Research at the Robotics Institute at CMU involves developing new computer-based medical devices to improve patient outcomes through increased speed and accuracy in surgical procedures.

Sports in Pittsburgh

Steelers game at Three Rivers Stadium

JBL

The Steelers and their Fans.
Three Rivers Stadium seats
thousands of enthusiastic
Steelers fans with their "ter-
rible towels", and those that
don't fit in the stadium cel-
ebrate in the parking lot.

Don Robinson

Out at second base

The Pittsburgh Pirates have been an institution in Pittsburgh since the early 1900s when games were played at Exhibition Park on the site of the present Three Rivers Stadium. Under the new ownership the Pirates are entering the 21st century with a new vigor and excitement.

JBL

Three Rivers Stadium during a Pittsburgh Pirates baseball game

The Roberto Clemente sculpture (S. Wagner) was dedicated at the 1994 All Star game, bringing back wonderful memories of "Play Ball" at Forbes Field (1953), in Oakland. Pittsburgh is planning on a baseball-only stadium with the allure of the Oakland ballpark.

JBL

Harold Corsini

Pittsburgh Penguins hockey games are played at the Civic Arena.

JBL

Pittsburgh neighborhoods play host to sports enthusiasts of the non-stadium sort. Here, the Great Race runs through Squirrel Hill, making its way to Point State Park.

JBL

JBL

The Thrift Drug Bike
Classic, held yearly, rides
its course through town,
down East Carson Street,
Southside, and climbs
Mt. Washington.

SLN

82

JBL

Fans offer cheers of support
on the Birmingham Bridge to
the Pittsburgh Marathon
runners, who make their way
through all of the city neighborhoods. Their run through
the Strip District leads thousands of runners across the
16th Street Bridge.

JBL

Hidden Treasures of the City

A quiet moment on the North Shore looking across the river to downtown Pittsburgh

Three Rivers Arts Festival
brings a variety of art to the
public all through the Golden
Triangle. Sculpture, paintings,
photography, video, food, and
music create an exciting atmo-
sphere every June.

JBL

Dan Kamin, renowned mime, attracts a following at Hartwood Acres.

JBL

Arts Festival food

JBL

Vintage Grand Prix

JBL

Three Rivers Regatta attracts hundreds of thousands of people from all over to gather on and around the rivers to see Formula One Racing, the Anything that Floats contest, and hot air balloons.

JBL

JBL

SLN

SLN

To the right is the Rotunda (c. 1900) at the historic Pennsylvania Station in downtown Pittsburgh, now an apartment complex. Below the Rotunda is the inside of the Croatian Church in Millvale which contains beautifully painted murals showing the migration of Eastern Europeans to America, struggles of the laboring classes, and World War I. To the left are three of a series of banners along 8th Avenue in Homestead, created by Robert Qualters, depicting the history of the area.

SLN

JBL

JBL

Reclamation

Doughboy sculpture (A. Newman, 1921) in Lawrenceville at Penn and Butler Streets

Celebration

Fireworks are a year-round display of pride in the city. Here they were set off during the holiday season.

Spirit

There is never a lack of spirit or enthusiasm in this town.

Penn Avenue in the Strip District

SLN

The Strip District

Fresh produce, meats, fish, and a variety of ethnic foods abound in markets and restaurants on Penn Avenue and Smallman Street.

Fresh produce

SLN

The jewels of Pittsburgh are its people. They are a blend of backgrounds, interests, and lifestyles that make Pittsburgh a great place to live and work.

91

Light -up Night

JBL

Light-up Night at Point State Park

SLN

Steel made Pittsburgh strong in the past. Now the land once occupied by steel mills is developed for technology centers and other businesses. This blast furnace was torn down in 1983.

JBL

Pittsburgh from the West End overlook

The Point c. 1900

Smokey City Beach, 1908

A nostalgic look back as Pittsburgh entered the 20th century.

The photographs in this book are primarily those done by Joel B. Levinson and Susan L. Nega. A credit line next to a picture of JBL refers to Joel, and a credit line of SLN refers to Susan. Together they manage J.B. Jeffers Ltd. which markets PITTSBURGHSCAPE photographic products such as books, The Pittsburghscape Calendar, postcards, note cards, prints, and related items containing Pittsburgh images and maps. The company also sells the reproduction rights from its large stock photography library.

Additional contributors to this book are Norman Schumm, Donald Robinson, Mary Jo Dowling, and Richard Kolson. Some photographs have been made available through the Pennsylvania Room of the Carnegie Library.

The introduction was written by Robert Gangewere, editor of the Carnegie Magazine.

The driving force behind the publication of this book was Joel's wife, Toba, to whom it is dedicated with everlasting love.

All photographs in this book are available for purchase as limited edition prints. For information call 412-421-7916, or visit our web site at http://www. pittsburghscape.com/